I Can Make a Water Dance

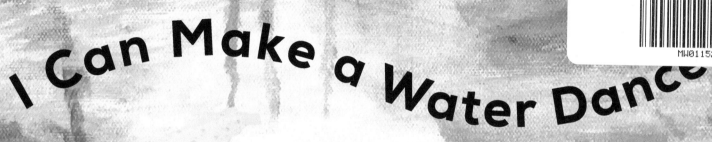

Written and Illustrated by
Karen Diaz Ensanian

Dedicated to all who love dance.

Note: This book was intended to motivate the making of dances inspired by the movement of water. It is always advised that children be supervised when in or near water.

ISBN: 978-0-9963919-1-7
Library of Congress Control Number: 2020925535

Published 2021 in the USA by Equus Potentia Publishing, LLC
www.equuspotentiapublishing.com

EQUUS POTENTIA
PUBLISHING

Printed in the United States of America

Foreword

My goal was to create a book that helps children make connections with the natural world and see themselves as part of it. By observing images of water and translating them into their own bodies, children begin to make dance.

Young dancers will explore dance movement guided by new vocabulary and poetry. They will therefore develop a greater understanding of water, and of their own bodies, while internalizing a deep love of the world they live in.

The journey of this book follows the path of the water cycle from evaporation, condensation, precipitation and collection. Throughout the book, dancer images are paired with a question that sets readers on the path to creating their own water dances.

Mist

I rise, float, hover.
I become light and free.

Can you find another way
to move like mist?

As the mist warms and water evaporates, where can it go?

Clouds

I sail, puff, and grow.
I cluster, then trail.

Can you find another way to move like clouds?

As clouds gather and grow heavier, what happens?

Storm Cloud

I grow heavy and dark as I rise. Lightning shoots from my center as my wind blows fearlessly.

Can you find another way to move like a storm cloud?

As the storm clouds grow too heavy, what happens to the water?

Rain

*I shower and soak the ground.
I pound down in sheets.
I drizzle gentle drops on the earth.*

Can you find another way to move like rain?

As it rains, what can the water create?

Puddle

*I collect and sit on streets and rocks.
I am a playground for children
or a drinking place for birds.
I jiggle, splatter, grow and shrink!*

Can you find another way to move like a puddle?

As the rainstorm ends, what happens when the sun comes out and shines through the tiny drops still in the sky?

Rainbow

I slowly appear arching, curving, bridging, with crystal colors, then, gently fade into the mist.

Can you find another way to move like a rainbow?

As it gets colder and colder
and the water in the sky falls,
what happens?

Snow

I flutter, swirl, and drift in a
flurry of flakes.
In the icy cold, I freeze into
a blanket heavy and white.

Can you find another way
to move like snow?

When it is freezing, what happens to the rivers and dripping water?

On cold days I tightly freeze into shapes and sparkle in the light. I float in chunks upon the river and drip from rocks.

Can you find another way to move like ice?

When the air warms, what happens to the snow?

Stream

*I melt, trickle, swerve.
I curl over rocks.*

Can you find another way to move like a stream?

Where do the streams go?

River

I rush, flow, and roll in a path, racing, splashing, and meandering towards the ocean or a lake.

Can you find another way to move like a river?

What happens when the river water drops suddenly on its way to the ocean?

Waterfall

I tumble, and pour over the edge, bubbling, leaping, cascading.

Can you find another way to move like a waterfall?

Where else can river water go?

Lake

*I ripple and shimmer in the light.
Calm and smooth, I mirror the sky.*

Can you find another way to
move like a lake?

What happens if there is an underground lake near very hot rocks?

Geyser

I boil, steam, and burst.
I vent out of the cracks in the earth and shoot into the air.

Can you find another way to move like a geyser?

What is the biggest body of water where many rivers go?

Ocean

I swell and crash on the beach, waves spraying.

Can you find another way to move like the ocean?

Water from the ground, puddles, snow, lakes, geysers, streams, rivers and oceans evaporate, rising to make clouds. Rain and snow is the water returning to the earth.

It's a journey that never ends.

What a water dance!

I Can Make a Water Dance

Drip

Drizzle
Drops

Land

Pour

Trail

Shower

Soak

Splatter

Swerve

Tumble

Grow

Roll

Freeze

Shoot

Arch

Curl

Curve

Float

Flutter

Mirror

Hover

Steam

Swirl

Crash

Drift

Melt

Swell

Blow

Rise

Splash

Sail

Bend

Flow

Burst

What will
your water dance
look like?

Tips for parents and teachers

How to create a dance:

1. Decide on the theme of your dance.

2. Select a variety of action words and different ways to do them that help you illustrate your theme.

3. You can use different body parts, qualities, feelings, pathways, sizes and levels. You can be in solos, partners, or groups, and use music and words.

4. Create a beginning and an ending.

5. Share your dance with others. Enjoy!

For more ideas go to **www.icanmakeadance.com** and follow us at **@icanmakeadance**

Acknowledgements and Thanks

To Armand who I owe the greatest thanks for his patience, unwavering technical and artistic support of my dreams.

To Carla for her editorial and artistic support.

To Lisa whose design expertise made this project a reality.

To Matthew, Natasha, and baby Zuleika for always encouraging me with great advice.

To Danny who always is cheering me on with kindness and grace.

To my mother Jeanne who always showed great enthusiasm.

To Maryna for her painting inspiration and loving guidance.

To my DEL colleagues for their feedback, care, and support: John-Mario, Diane, Mary, Erin, and Dawn

And last but not least, a big thank you to my beautiful dancers without whom this book would not have been possible: Elise, Elaina, Ethan, Plum, Henry, Ellie and Arthur!

K.D.E.

Karen Diaz Ensanian has devoted her professional life to the dance education of people of all ages. Her extensive experience includes over twenty years as an early childhood educator.

Karen started her early career in New York City as dancer with several choreographers, including dancing as a founding member with the Alvin Ailey Repertory Company. She later received her M.A. in Dance from The Ohio State University and then taught for nineteen years as Director of Creative Movement at The Episcopal School in The City of New York. In recent years Karen facilitated Dance Education Laboratory professional development workshops for teachers with the Department of Education in New York City.

At the same time, Karen began teaching herself to paint as a foundation for illustrating a children's dance education book.

Karen currently lives with her husband in NYC where she raised two children.

CPSIA information can be obtained
at www.ICGtesting.com
Printed in the USA
BVHW091909160523
664274BV00013B/62